Missing!

Written by Roderick Hunt
Illustrated by Alex Brychta

OXFORD
UNIVERSITY PRESS

Nadim had a hamster.
He called it Jaws.

"Jaws is a funny name for
a hamster," said Biff.

Nadim put Jaws in his cage, but
he forgot to shut the cage door.

Jaws got out of the cage and
ran off.

Nadim saw the cage was open.

"Oh no!" he said.

Nadim was upset.

"Jaws has run off," said Nadim.

"We can look for him," said Biff.

They looked and looked.

Biff looked under the sink.

Chip looked in the fridge.

Nadim looked under the
cupboard.

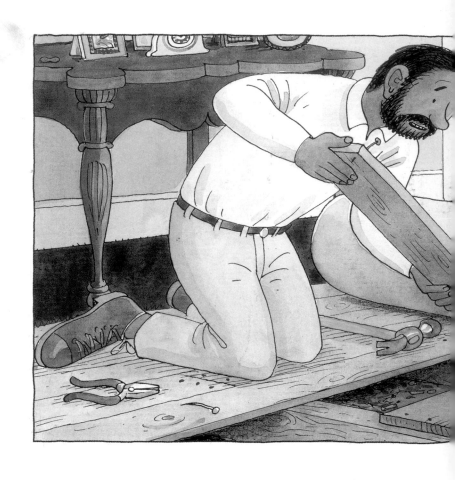

Nadim's dad looked under
the floor.

"Is Jaws down here?" he said.

Then Chip had an idea.

"Let's get Floppy. He can help us."

Sniff, sniff, went Floppy.

Sniff, sniff!   SNIFF! SNIFF!

"Look in there," said Chip.

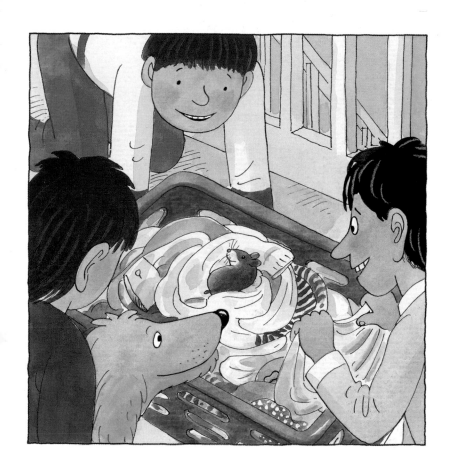

Jaws was in the clothes basket.

He had made a nest.

"Look!" said Nadim. "You can
see why I called him Jaws."

Talk about the story

Odd one out

Which two things don't begin with the same sound as the
'**h**' at the beginning of '**h**amster'?